DO I HAVE A HOUSE FOR YOU!

by

HARRIETT BRONSON

BEAUTIFUL SPLIT-LEVEL FOR SALE

PRICE/STERN/SLOAN
Publishers, Inc., Los Angeles
1980

DEDICATION

To my son Tony and daughter Suzanne
and
To the many people who have chosen to give up food and clothing for shelter
and
To the realtors everywhere who rack their brains creating the "brilliant" copy for ads such as these.

Illustrations by Edwin Puissant

Copyright© 1980 by Harriett Bronson
Published by Price/Stern/Sloan Publishers, Inc.
410 North La Cienega Boulevard, Los Angeles, California 90048

Printed in the United States of America. All rights reserved. No part of this publication may be reproduced, stored in a retrieval system or transmitted, in any form or by any means, electronic, mechanical, photocopying, recording or otherwise, without the prior written permission of the publishers.

ISBN: 0-8431-0155-5
PSS!® is a registered trademark of Price/Stern/Sloan Publishers, Inc.

INTRODUCTION

We've all been intrigued by impressive sounding real estate ads that colorfully promise a dream home in the sky. These sales pitches conjure up tranquil images of lush lawns, blooming gardens, and perfect rows of white picket fences . . . The American Dream only a phone call away!

Unfortunately, in the real world of leaky plumbing, mortgage rates, and crabgrass, there's always more (or less) than meets the eye. Like a new car, a new home can turn into a lemon upon closer inspection.

So, to help "the buyer beware," this guide presents a look at what nightmares might lie behind the beautifully-described dreams.

READING THESE ADS

Reading a real estate ad is tricky business at best. Unless you're familiar with the language in the ads, you're in trouble (confusing your "bd.'s" with your "ba.'s" can lead to embarrassing situations). To acquaint you with real estate jargon, here's a condensed glossary of commonly used terms:

ARTIST'S CONCEPTION
What someone hoped it would look like.

BACK TO NATURE
Includes mosquitos.

"BY APPOINTMENT ONLY"
"We don't want you seeing this turkey without a salesman."

COUNTRY CLUB ATMOSPHERE
Nosey neighbors.

COUNTRY LIVING
A parcel with a patch of grass between the slabs of concrete.

DYNAMITE LOCATION
Neighboring hills being blasted for freeway.

ENCLOSED GROUNDS; FENCED YARD
Dangerous neighborhood.

ESTATE
It costs $20,000 more than it's worth.

FIXER UPPER
A $60,000 house needing $80,000 worth of repairs.

FROM $60,000
Upwards of $90,000

GARDEN KITCHEN
Weeds come right up to the door.

INVESTMENT PROPERTY
   Impossible to live on; impossible to build on.
LUSH GARDEN
   Winos in the flower beds.
MAXIMUM SECURITY
   An old man with a rusty gun sleeps by the front gate.
NEAR SCHOOLS
   Vandalism rampant.
OLD WORLD ATMOSPHERE
   Dark, dusty, and drafty.
ONE OF A KIND
   Architect didn't have the gall to build two.
OWNER MUST SELL
   Foreclosure imminent . . . he can't meet the payments either.
RIVIERA LIFESTYLE
   Next door to a Buick plant.
RUSTIC
   Ramshackle enough to tear down but too new to condemn.
SECLUDED
   Deserted. Impossible to find. No road in.
SPECTACULAR VIEW
   On a clear day you can see the neighbors.
TOWNHOUSES
   $80,000 tenements.
WET BAR
   The bar is small and it leaks.
WINE CELLAR
   Damp basement.
WOOD SHAKE ROOF
   Built on an earthquake fault.

GARDENER'S DELIGHT!

Dig in and enjoy! Live like a country squire. For those who love to putter in the garden. Earthy, full of charm. Nature's way of saying "Hi". Modestly priced at $60,000. Hurry – bargain won't last.

VINE REALTY INC.

CREATIVE RETREAT

Hip and artistic environment – the pad for the REAL you! Gorgeous two bedroom, two bath. Excellent view – canals, water, ducks and boats. European ambience. Artistic types only – rush before the word gets out! Priced to move – $47,500.

TAKEM REALTY

CLOSE TO EVERYTHING!

Watch the world go by – Smashing View! This 2 bdrm. colonial w/picture window is frwy. close to dwntwn. Anxious owner has reduced price to $52,500.

OFFRAMP REALTY

FOR COUNTRY SQUIRES!

Country living at its best. Lo. maint., 2 bd., 1 Early American ba. Awaken to the sounds of nature. "Back to basics" lifestyle. Zoned for animals. A steal at $88,000.

SUNSHINE REALTY

NEED SPACE?

Unique, authentic Spanish estate – for seekers who need their own "space". Comfy old-world atmosphere. 15 bdr., 5 ba., den, high ceilings. 3 fplc., Lrge. living rm., acres of arches. Defies description! 2 stunning stories w/lots of taste. Priced to shout about at $2,950,000.

FIXER WITH A FUTURE!

A gem in the rough. Opportunity of a lifetime for the creative with vision and talent. Open, airy, and rustic. 2 bd., 2½ ba., open beams. A decorator's delight. Needs paint. Only $75,000.

PICASSO REALTY

THE OCEAN IN YOUR BACKYARD!

Carefree living. Exciting beachfront. Pick up and go on a moment's notice. A real charmer w/hi ceiling, 2 bd., 2 ba., bay window. Great for the weekend surfer. A steal at $155,000.

SEA SHELL REALTY

CUTE 'N' COZY COTTAGE!

Touchy, Feely, Friendly Cottage. Everything close by. A charming love nest for together types. Many amenities: wdbrng frplc., natural flrs. 1 bd. 1 ba. Only $55,000.

CRAMMIT REALTY

EXCITING!

Secluded hide-away for those on the way up. 3 bd., 2 ba., den, skylight. High on a hill with a view of forever! No frwy. noise; clean air. Step up to spectacular living. $160,000.

EAGLE REALTY

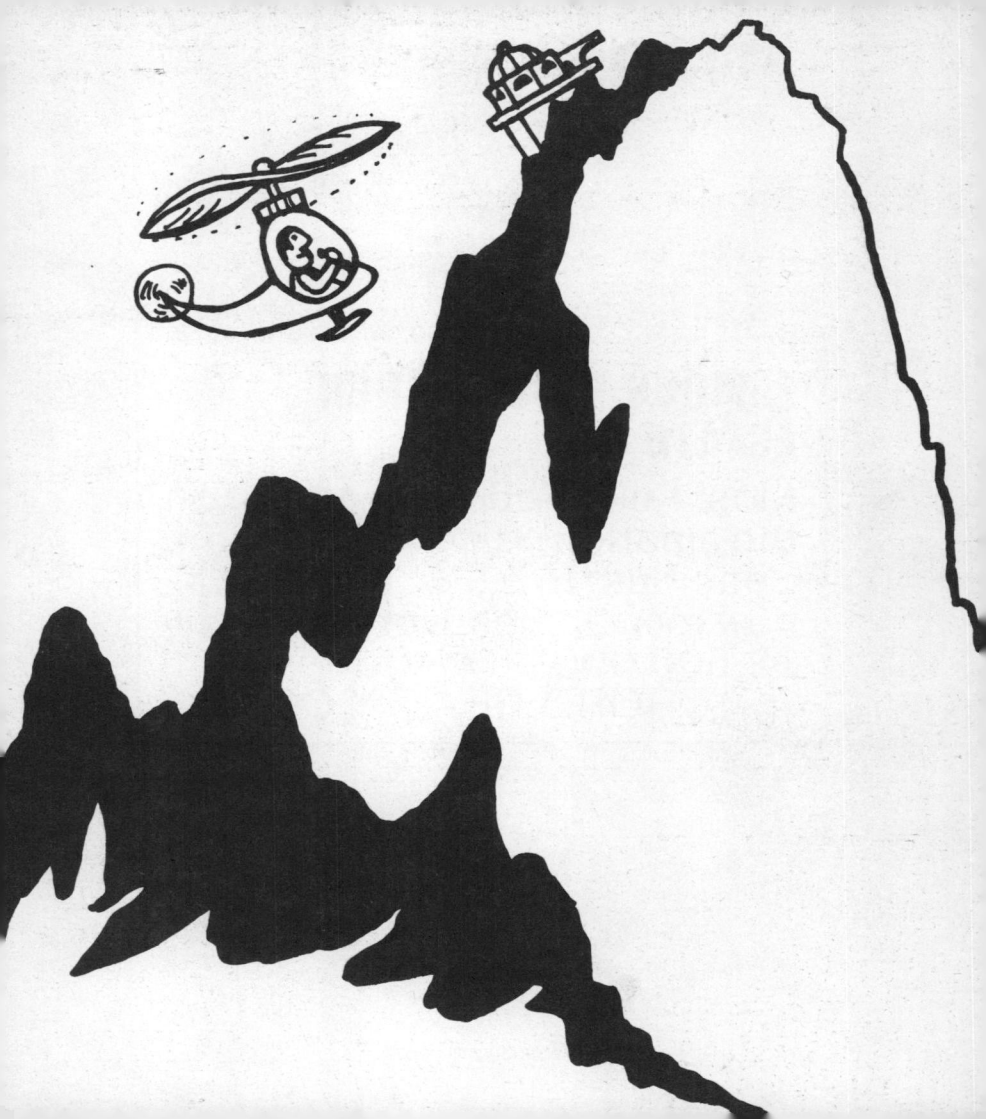

FAMOUS ENTERTAINER'S ESTATE

Most talked about property on the market! Unique design. Spacious rms., 5 bd., 7 ba., new roof, arches, ivory walkway. $2,500,000.

CHORD REALTY CO.

OLD WORLD CHARM

Maintenance free, worry free. Built to last! Wine cellar, observation decks. Subterranean play rooms. Select residence. Room for pets. Maximum security. $1,450,000.
FRIENDLY HOME REALTY

SCHOOL BUS STOPS 4 DOORS AWAY!

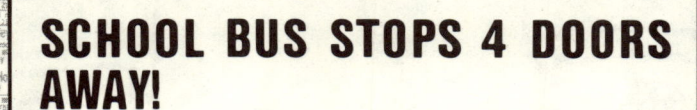

For the active family! Think young, feel young, suburban living. 4 bd., 2½ ba., versatile fireplace; New chimney. Children in neighborhood. A hop, skip, and jump from playground & rec. facilities. $89,500.

LIVE RENT FREE!

Mature couple needed to manage large complex. Elegant, friendly atmosphere. Spacious 1 bd., 1½ ba. Relax by rumpus area and fully heated pool. Step up to a new life!

MODERN REALTY AND MANAGEMENT

This book is published by

PRICE/STERN/SLOAN
Publishers, Inc., Los Angeles

whose other splendid titles include such literary classics as:

THE LEGAL GUIDE TO MOTHER GOOSE ($2.50)

MURPHY'S LAW AND OTHER REASONS WHY THINGS GO WRONG! ($2.50)

MURPHY'S LAW/BOOK TWO ($2.50)

THE WORLD'S WORST MORON JOKES ($1.50)

THE WORLD'S WORST KNOCK KNOCK JOKES ($1.50)

THE WORLD'S WORST GOLF JOKES ($1.50)

They are available wherever books are sold or may be ordered directly from the publisher by sending check or money order for the full price of each title plus 50 cents for handling and mailing. For a complete list of titles send a *stamped, self-addressed envelope* to:

PRICE/STERN/SLOAN *Publishers, Inc.*
410 North La Cienega Boulevard, Los Angeles, California 90048